Contents

KU-032-563

Unsolved mysteries

For centuries, people have been puzzled and fascinated by mysterious places, creatures and events. Is there really a monster in Loch Ness? Did the lost city of Atlantis ever exist? Are crop circles messages from aliens, or simply clever hoaxes? Is there life on Mars or Venus? Why did the dinosaurs suddenly die out?

Some of these mysteries have baffled scientists, who have spent years trying to find the answers. But just how far can science go? Can it really explain the unexplained? Are there some mysteries which science simply cannot solve? Read on, and try to make up your own mind ...

When you stand next to a dinosaur skeleton, it seems amazing that such huge animals could have been wiped out.

Can
Scienc
Solve?

ery

D

e

Heinemann
L I B R A R Y

www.heinemann.co.uk/library
Visit our website to find out more information about **Heinemann Library** books.

To order:
 Phone 44 (0) 1865 888066
 Send a fax to 44 (0) 1865 314091
Visit the Heinemann Bookshop at www.heinemann.co.uk/library to browse our catalogue and order online.

First published in Great Britain by Heinemann Library,
Halley Court, Jordan Hill, Oxford OX2 8EJ,
a division of Reed Educational and Professional Publishing Ltd.
Heinemann is a registered trademark of Reed Educational & Professional Publishing Limited.

OXFORD MELBOURNE AUCKLAND
JOHANNESBURG BLANTYRE GABORONE
IBADAN PORTSMOUTH NH (USA) CHICAGO

Designed by AMR
Illustrations by Art Construction
Origination by Ambassador Litho Ltd
Printed in China

ISBN 0 431 01623 2 (hardback)   ISBN 0 431 01648 8 (paperback)
06 05 04 03 02   07 06 05 04 03
10 9 8 7 6 5 4 3 2 1   10 9 8 7 6 5 4 3 2 1

British Library Cataloguing in Publication Data

Oxlade, Chris
  Can science solve the mystery of the death of the dinosaurs?
  1.Dinosaurs – Juvenile literature 2.Extinction (Biology) –
  Juvenile literature
  I.Title II.Wallace, Holly, 1961– III.The death of the dinosaurs
  567.9

Acknowledgements
The Publishers would like to thank the following for permission to reproduce photographs: Bruce Coleman Collection: p28; Corbis: pp4, 15; Mary Evans Picture Library: pp6, 7; Natural History Museum/J Sibbick: p11; Oxford Scientific Films: p27, Science Photo Library: pp8, 10, 13, 14, 17, 18, 20, 23, 24, 25, 26, 29; Will & Dent McIntyre: p19.

Cover photograph reproduced with permission of Science Photo Library.

Every effort has been made to contact copyright holders of any material reproduced in this book. Any omissions will be rectified in subsequent printings if notice is given to the Publisher.

Any words appearing in the text in bold, **like this**, are explained in the Glossary.

Big and small

Dinosaurs are famous for their massive size. It's true that some dinosaurs were staggeringly big. Animals such as *Diplodocus* grew up to 27 metres long and weighed 70 or 80 tonnes. That's twice as long and twice as heavy as a fully-loaded articulated truck. But many species of dinosaurs were no bigger than cats or dogs, and some were as small as chickens. Some dinosaurs had armoured plates in their skin and weapons on their tails for self-defence. Not all dinosaurs were fierce, either! Many were **herbivores**, meaning that they ate only plants.

*The **carnivore** Tyrannosaurus evolved in the Cretaceous period.*

Evolution of the dinosaurs

At the end of Palaeozoic era, 250 million years ago, there were no dinosaurs. The land was ruled by other types of reptiles. These reptiles evolved into turtles, a group of reptiles that looked like small mammals, and a group of reptiles called the **archosaurs**. The archosaurs evolved into different groups, too, including marine reptiles, flying reptiles (called pterosaurs), crocodiles and the first dinosaurs.

By the end of the Triassic period, 205 million years ago, the early dinosaurs had evolved into many groups, and they dominated the land. Their **evolution** continued for another 140 million years. Some dinosaur species became rare or died out completely and new ones evolved. By the end of the Cretaceous period, horned and duck-billed dinosaurs were the most common.

The dinosaurs' world

The dinosaurs dominated the world for a long time, so it's not surprising that it changed a great deal during that time. When the dinosaurs first evolved in the Triassic period, there was just one big land mass, called Pangaea, which means 'all Earth'. Since then, Pangaea has gradually split apart, creating the continents that we know today. Most of this land movement took place when the dinosaurs were alive, and it had a huge effect on the conditions on Earth.

Over millions of years, Pangaea split apart to form the continents we know today.

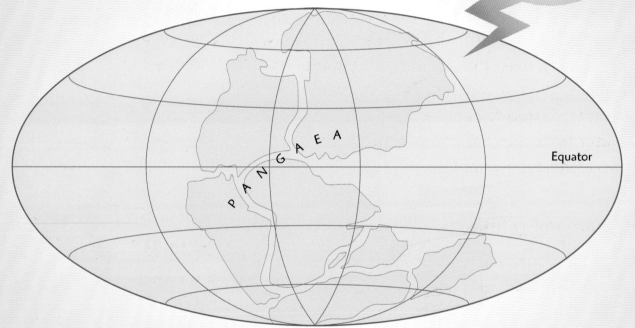

Changing climates

Climate is the pattern of weather that a place has. The world's climates have always changed slowly, with periods of warmer climates and then cooler climates. During the time that the dinosaurs lived, the climates changed as Pangaea split up. The drifting continents affected the climates of the whole world, and each piece of land slowly moved through different climates.

Pterosaurs were flying reptiles. They were not dinosaurs, but they died out at the same time.

In the middle of the Cretaceous period, the Earth was very warm, with **sub-tropical** conditions almost everywhere. Forests grew on land near the Earth's poles, which have ice-caps today, even though it was completely dark for months on end. Then, towards the end of the Cretaceous, the climate started to cool again. Sea levels began to fall, as sea water froze and became part of the ice caps, and some places started to have proper seasons.

Changing plants

When the dinosaurs first appeared, plants were very different from today. They were mostly ferns, mosses, horsetails and some conifers. There were no flowering plants. During the Jurassic period, conifers evolved into pines, redwoods and araucaria (monkey puzzle trees), and formed huge forests. By the Cretaceous period, flowering plants dominated the plant world, as they do today. The plant-eating dinosaurs had to adapt to eat the new plants that evolved.

Other animals

*Dinosaurs were not the only animals that lived on Earth at the time. There were many other species of **reptiles**, such as the flying pterosaurs and the swimming ichthyosaurs and plesiosaurs. There were also fish, birds, small furry mammals and insects. Many of these were prey for the smaller **carnivorous** dinosaurs.*

Fossil evidence

We only know that dinosaurs existed, and understand how they lived and what their world was like, from their remains and the remains of other animals and plants. These remains are called **fossils**. Fossils have been found in layers of **sedimentary rock** in every continent.

What are fossils?

Fossils form when the remains of an animal or plant become buried under **sediment**, such as mud or **silt**. The flesh and other soft parts rot away quickly, leaving just the hard bones and teeth. In the wet sediment, **minerals** gradually replace the bones and teeth, turning them into rock. Over millions of years, the sediment turns into sedimentary rock, such as sandstone. If the rock is lifted to the surface and **eroded** away, the fossils are exposed.

Dinosaur skeletons are normally found in many pieces. Putting them together is a painstaking task.

This book tells you about the death of the dinosaurs. It looks at what the dinosaurs were, at when, where and how they lived, and at how we know about them. Then it examines the theories about why they died.

What was the death of the dinosaurs?

You must have heard of the dinosaurs. They were the most amazing group of animals that ever existed. Some of the dinosaurs were the largest animals that have ever lived on land, weighing up to twenty times as much as an elephant. They dominated the world for more than 160 million years. That's more than a hundred times longer than humans have existed. That is why it's such a mystery that, 65 million years ago, the dinosaurs completely disappeared. Every dinosaur alive at the time died.

What caused the death of these animals? It's a question that anybody who has read about dinosaurs asks. But it's not an easy question to answer. They died out a very long time ago, so finding the answer means trying to discover what happened in the distant past. Some people think the dinosaurs were wiped out by a massive meteorite, and the change in weather conditions that followed. Others think they just died out naturally.

Without science, we would not even know that the dinosaurs existed. So is there anything science can do to help us find out why they disappeared? This book will help you to answer that question.

Beginnings of a mystery

Two hundred years ago, nobody knew that the dinosaurs, or hundreds of other **extinct** species, ever existed. So they had no idea that these amazing creatures suddenly died out. Scientists also thought that the Earth was a few thousand years old at most.

Early finds

People have been finding dinosaur bones for hundreds of years. The first find of a dinosaur **fossil** that we know about comes from 1677, when Robert Plot of Oxford University in Britain was sent a piece of a large thigh bone. He thought it came from an elephant brought to Britain by the Romans, or from an extremely large human. We now know that it came from a dinosaur called *Megalosaurus*.

British scientist Sir Richard Owen (1804-92) built some of the first dinosaur models.

The first proper scientific studies of dinosaurs were made in the 1820s. Gideon Mantell, a British doctor, found some large fossil teeth and bones. He concluded that they came from a giant **reptile**, which he named *Iguanodon*. William Buckland of Oxford University also studied some fossil bones. He worked out that they must have come from a huge, meat-eating reptile which he named *Megalosaurus*, meaning 'giant lizard'. These scientists had no reason to believe that similar animals were not still living in some unexplored part of the world.

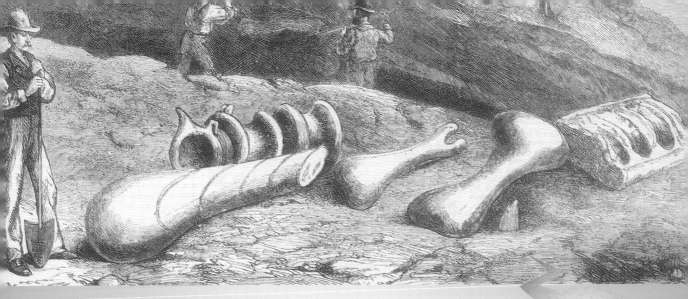

In the 1840s, another British scientist, Richard Owen, studied all the fossils of large reptiles found at the time. He found many similar features and reached the important conclusion that they all belonged to one group of reptiles that no longer lived on Earth. He gave the group the name *Dinosauria*, meaning 'terrible lizards'. Soon there was a huge amount of interest in dinosaurs.

How old were the fossils?

At the same time, **geologists** were realizing that the rocks they studied must be extremely old. They saw huge mountains being **eroded** slowly to form **sediment**, and new rocks forming as the sediment fell to the bottom of rivers and lakes. They concluded that thick beds of **sedimentary rocks** must have taken millions of years to form. This meant that the fossils found in them must have come from creatures that lived millions of years ago.

In the early 20th century, a way of calculating the exact age of rocks was devised. It worked by measuring how radioactive the rocks were. No dinosaur fossils were found in rocks younger than 65 million years, meaning that no dinosaurs existed after that time. So what had happened to the dinosaurs?

Geological time

Before we can look at the theories about why the dinosaurs died, we need to understand more about how they lived and what the Earth was like at the time. This was a very long time ago, so first we need to understand how **geologists** and **palaeontologists** measure time in the distant past, and learn some of the jargon they use.

The age of the Earth

The Earth is very, very old! It was formed 4600 million years ago from the dust and gas left over after the Sun was born. At first it was just a lump of red-hot rock. Life is thought to have started from the chemicals in the oceans about 3500 million years ago. For thousands of millions of years, the only forms of life were very simple single-celled organisms.

About 550 million years ago, more complicated forms of plants and animals evolved. Some forms started to colonize the land. The dinosaurs evolved about 225 million years ago and died out 65 million years ago. Humans evolved only within the last million years. We have been on the Earth for only a tiny fraction of its life!

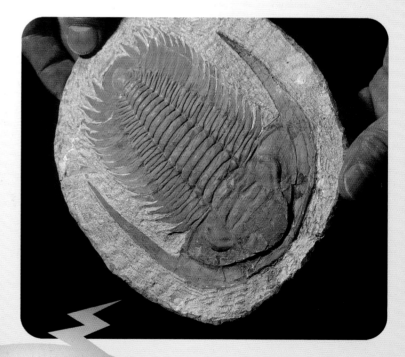

This is a trilobite fossil. It would have lived in the sea about 550 million years ago.

Geological time

Geologists and palaeontologists use the geological timescale to measure time. They have divided the time since the formation of the Earth into chunks and given each one a name. Each chunk begins and ends when the **fossils** from the time show that a major change took place on Earth.

Geological time is divided into two huge chunks, called aeons. They are the Precambrian and Phanerozoic. The Phanerozoic is divided into three eras. They are the Palaeozoic (when life lived mainly in the seas), the Mesozoic (when the dinosaurs ruled), and the Cenozoic (from the death of the dinosaurs to the present day). Each of these eras is divided into smaller chunks called periods. The Mesozoic, when the dinosaurs lived, is divided into the Triassic, the Jurassic and the Cretaceous periods.

The KT boundary

The dinosaurs died out around the end of the Cretaceous period and the beginning of the Tertiary, which was the first period in the Cenozoic era. This time is known as the **KT boundary** *– K stands for 'Cretaceous' (because C is used for another period, the 'Carboniferous') and T stands for 'Tertiary'.*

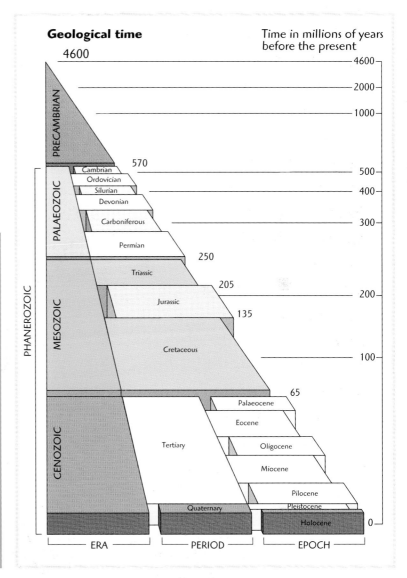

What were the dinosaurs like?

Dinosaurs were **reptiles**. They shared some of the characteristics of lizards, crocodiles, snakes and other modern reptiles. For example, we think dinosaurs had tough, scaly skin and their young hatched out of eggs. But there was one important difference. All dinosaurs had legs that came straight down from their bodies, rather than out and then down, as the legs of modern-day lizards and crocodiles do. This meant that dinosaurs could stand upright and walk, either on two legs or four.

How many species?

So far **palaeontologists** have identified about 700 different species of dinosaurs. This is not very many, considering that there are thousands of species of birds and mammals alive today. So there are probably hundreds more dinosaur species waiting to be discovered. Not all these species lived at the same time. Different species were constantly evolving and dying out during the 160 million years that the dinosaurs walked the Earth.

An artist's impression of the Earth during the Cretaceous period.

Information from fossils

Fossils can tell us a huge amount. Fossil bones allow **palaeontologists** to work out the size and shape of dinosaurs, and how they moved about. Fossil footprints tell us that some dinosaurs walked on two legs. Rare fossil eggs have been found in groups, which tells us that some dinosaurs lived in colonies, like seabirds do today. And rare fossil skin tells us what dinosaurs looked like.

But fossils can't tell us everything. Only a tiny fraction of all the animals that die turn into fossils. It's estimated that we only have fossils of one per cent of all the species that ever lived. So there are many gaps in what palaeontologists call the fossil record. There may have been hundreds of species of dinosaurs that we will never know about.

A fossilized dinosaur footprint in New Mexico, USA.

More evidence

Fossils of plants from the dinosaur age tell us how the Earth looked at the time and how the climate gradually changed. Matching fossils from different continents tells us how the super-continent of Pangaea fitted together.

The dinosaur extinction

Extinction means the death of all the individual animals or plants in a species. This means that the species will never live again. Throughout the history of life on Earth – from 3500 millions years ago to the present day – millions of species have evolved and then become **extinct**. **Fossil** records show us that very few species have existed for more than a million years. In fact, 99 per cent of all the species that have ever lived on Earth are now extinct.

Adapt or die

Species normally become extinct because environmental conditions change. For example, a species that lives only in a certain area could die out as its **habitat** gradually turns to desert, or because a new species of **predator** evolves and feeds on it. These changes normally take millions of years. Some species naturally evolve or adapt to living in the new conditions, perhaps turning into completely new species. Others do not evolve quickly enough and die out.

Fossil records also show that there are periods in geological time when thousands of species have died out in a very short space of time. **Palaeontologists** call these periods 'extinction events' or 'mass extinctions'.

The KT boundary event

The most famous mass extinction happened at the **KT boundary** – the end of the Cretaceous period and the beginning of the Tertiary period. Palaeontologists call it the 'KT boundary event'. Every species of dinosaur that was alive at the time died.

16

Unfortunately, we cannot date rocks accurately enough to tell how long the KT boundary event lasted. Some scientists think it lasted as little as a few days, others that it lasted for more than a million years. So although people say that the dinosaurs all died at exactly the same time, we cannot prove that this was the case.

Other species that died

It was not only the dinosaurs that died out during the KT boundary event. Many other creatures died too, including some species of lizards, sharks, birds and marsupials. All species of plesiosaurs and mesosaurs became extinct. So did the ammonites, which had lived in the oceans for hundreds of millions of years. In fact, about 75 per cent of all the animal species died. Those that survived included most species of fish, amphibians and mammals.

*This is a skeleton of a **carnivorous** dinosaur that lived in the seas over 65 million years ago. It is over 8 m long.*

The impact theory

The first and most famous theory about what caused the death of the dinosaurs is that conditions were changed dramatically by a massive meteorite smashing into the Earth. This is called the 'extra-terrestrial impact theory' or 'catastrophic theory'.

A meteorite is a piece of space debris that crashes into the Earth's surface. Some meteorites are made of rock, some are made mainly of iron, and some are a mixture of the two. The pieces of debris are bits left over from the formation of the **Solar System**. Hundreds of pieces of debris collide with the Earth every day. Most are very small and burn up as they enter the Earth's **atmosphere** at speeds of up to 70 kilometres per second. Occasionally, larger pieces get through the atmosphere and create impact **craters** in the ground.

When a large meteorite landed in Siberia in 1908 it flattened trees for 50 km around.

Collision effects

What would have happened if a huge meteorite had hit the Earth at the time of the dinosaurs? Here's the theory. The meteorite was very big indeed, probably about 10 kilometres across – the same size as a major city. It hurtled down through the atmosphere at 50 kilometres a second, leaving a bright streak across the sky, and smashed into the shallow sea.

The impact caused an explosion equivalent to 100 million million million tonnes of TNT exploding at once. That's an explosion more powerful than if all the world's nuclear weapons detonated at the same time. It created a crater more than ten kilometres deep and hundreds of kilometres across. A **supersonic** shock wave blasted out from the site, setting light to forests, and giant waves called tsunamis spread across the sea, flooding low-lying coastal areas for thousands of kilometres.

The impact, shock wave and flooding killed thousands of dinosaurs, but most died because of the climate change that followed ...

An impact winter

The meteorite impact threw millions of tonnes of dust high into the Earth's atmosphere. This dust slowly spread around the upper atmosphere, creating a dusty blanket that blocked out the Sun's heat and light. Over the next few months, the atmosphere cooled by as much as 20 °C. The weather became very cold and plants could not grow properly. **Acid rain** fell from the clouds. The dinosaurs could never survive in these conditions.

Meteorite evidence

There is evidence that a huge meteorite hit the Earth at the end of the Cretaceous period. Layers of rock formed at the time contain chemicals that could have come from a meteorite, and a huge **crater** has been found in Mexico. This evidence supports the impact theory.

The iridium anomaly

Iridium is a type of metal. Only tiny amounts of it are found in the rocks of the Earth's crust. But meteorites often contain quite a lot of iridium. In several places around the world, **geologists** have found a layer of sedimentary rock, called mudstone, that contains amounts of iridium much higher than in other rocks. They call this layer the 'iridium **anomaly**'. Using **radiometric** techniques, the mudstone has been found to be about 65 million years old. That means it formed at the end of the Cretaceous, on the **KT boundary**, around the same time as the dinosaurs died out.

The Arizona Crater, USA, formed 22,000 years ago is obvious proof that big meteorites hit the Earth.

It is thought that a meteorite impact would have thrown dust rich in iridium into the **atmosphere**, which was then spread around the world. The dust eventually fell with rain, was washed down rivers and deposited in the bottom of lakes and seas, eventually forming the layer of iridium-rich rock.

Finding a crater

You can see from Earth that the surface of the Moon is covered in impact craters. Most of these were formed billions of years ago when meteorites hit the Moon. As many meteorites must have hit the Earth, but there are only a few impact craters visible, and none large enough to have been caused by a meteorite 10 kilometres across. Most craters have disappeared because they have been **eroded** away or covered over by new rock.

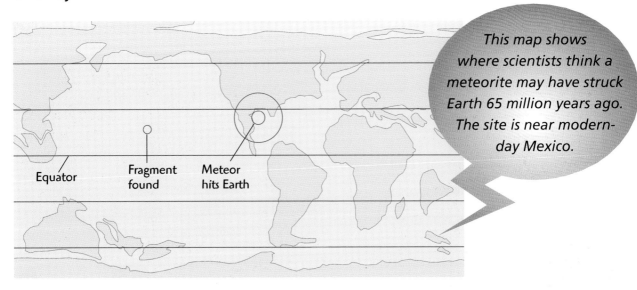

Equator   Fragment found   Meteor hits Earth

This map shows where scientists think a meteorite may have struck Earth 65 million years ago. The site is near modern-day Mexico.

But in the late 1990s, evidence was found of a vast crater, 240 kilometres wide, hidden under rocks on the Yucatan peninsula in Mexico. Named the Chicxulub Crater, it is in rocks formed in the late Cretaceous period. Rocks within a few hundred kilometres of the site contain a layer of glassy spherules (tiny balls of glass) that would have been formed by the intense heat of a meteorite impact. Is this the crater formed by the meteorite that killed the dinosaurs?

The habitat loss theory

The second main theory about the death of the dinosaurs is that they died out over millions of years because their **habitats** changed slowly and they could not adapt to survive in the conditions. This is called the 'habitat loss theory' or 'gradualist theory'.

Fossil records show that many species of dinosaur were dying out in the last 10 million years of the Cretaceous period. The numbers of individual skeletons of each species found from this period shows that this was the case. The number of different species was also declining.

Changing conditions

At the end of the Cretaceous period, the world's climate was slowly cooling. Sea levels were falling from being very high in the middle of the Cretaceous. These two factors led to a reduction in habitat for the dinosaurs.

Away from the equator, the lush vegetation began to be replaced by trees, and year-round warm weather was replaced by seasons with cold winters. The shallow seas near the coasts became land, and the land that was near the sea turned drier. The **herbivores** could no longer find the right food to eat. They began to die out. The **carnivores**, that ate the herbivores, also went hungry. The dinosaurs also had to fight other animals for food. All these changes were very slow. They took millions of years to happen.

The volcanic eruption of Mount St Helen's in the USA, sending a cloud of ash, gas and rock into the atmosphere.

Volcanic activity

Another theory is that climate change happened quite quickly, perhaps over thousands rather than millions of years, and was caused by volcanic activity.

In India there is a huge deposit of basalt called the Deccan Traps. Volcanoes must have been erupting there for tens of thousands of years to produce such a huge amount of basalt. It's thought that the volcanoes were formed by the drifting continents causing India to crash slowly into Asia. This happened at the time the dinosaurs died out. Eruptions on this scale would have sent gas and dust into the atmosphere, causing a climate change.

More extinction theories

We have looked at the two main theories that try to explain the death of the dinosaurs. They are the impact theory and **habitat** loss theory or gradualist theory. These two theories are sometimes called the 'bang' and 'whimper' theories! But there are dozens of other theories about why the dinosaurs died out, and hundreds of scientific papers have been written on the subject. Some of the theories are based on scientific evidence, but others are just plain silly!

Star activity

Two extinction theories are to do with the Sun and other stars. One is that a period of **sunspot** activity reduced the amount of heat reaching the Earth. This led to global cooling, which in turn led to climate change and the death of the dinosaurs. The other is that a nearby star exploded in a **supernova** – a massive explosion – that sent waves of deadly radiation towards the Earth.

A supernova happens when a star many times bigger than the Sun comes to the end of its life.

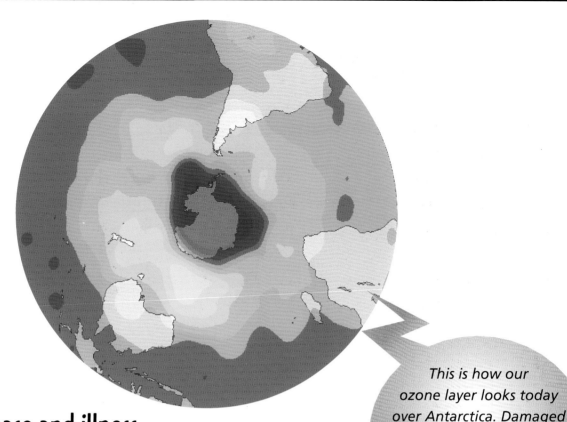

This is how our ozone layer looks today over Antarctica. Damaged ozone can mean climate change – as it may have done for the dinosaurs.

Disease and illness

There are also theories that the dinosaurs died out because of some sort of disease or illness. These include a plague that spread when sea levels fell and allowed dinosaurs that had **evolved** on different continents to meet, passing on the disease.

More theories

One recent theory is that plant-eating dinosaurs created huge amounts of **methane** gas. Big dinosaurs would have eaten hundreds of kilograms of plants every day, and would have passed lots of methane! This extra methane in the **atmosphere** would have damaged the **ozone layer**, which in turn allowed changes in climate and vegetation that disrupted the lives of dinosaurs. Other theories are that the dinosaurs died because of competition with caterpillars, or that mammals ate all their eggs.

Some of these theories are feasible, but there is no firm evidence for any of them.

Extinction through history

The **KT boundary** event, in which the dinosaurs were wiped out, was not the only time in history when hundreds of species have died out in a short space of time. There seem to have been several of these mass extinctions since the time when advanced life started, about 550 million years ago.

Fossil records show quite a regular pattern of mass extinctions, approximately every 26 million years for the last 250 million years. Five of these mass extinctions have been on a huge scale, when more than half of all the species alive at the time were killed off. Regular mass extinctions could be caused by some regular astronomical event, such as the Earth's path in space taking it across the path of a cloud of asteroids or comets.

The Permian extinction

The greatest mass extinction of all time happened at the end of the Permian period, the period before the Triassic (during which the dinosaurs evolved). It is called the 'Permian event', and it was catastrophic. About 95 per cent of all the species living at the time were wiped out. After the world had recovered, new species **evolved** from those that were left. These included the early dinosaurs, who took advantage of the lack of competition from other species.

Crocodiles evolved at the same time as the dinosaurs, but survived two mass extinctions.

Another extinction, this time not quite so large, separates the Triassic and Jurassic periods. This left the world ready to be dominated by the dinosaurs. So it's likely that the dinosaurs, who were killed off in a mass extinction, only became successful because of another mass extinction.

The coelacanth has been on Earth for 400 million years. It was thought to be extinct until 1932, when one was caught.

A modern extinction?

There's no reason to think that there will not be another mass extinction in the future. A few decades ago, a meteorite impact was thought to be something that only happened in the distant past. But in the last few years, the world's governments have begun to take the idea seriously. Organisations have been set up to watch out for any large asteroids on a collision course with the Earth. Whether we could stop one before it landed is a different matter!

In conclusion

So can science really solve the mystery of the death of the dinosaurs? It's not an easy job, because scientists have to find out what happened millions of years ago, and they only have rocks to look at!

Science tells us that the dinosaurs died in a relatively short space of time, compared to how long they inhabited the Earth. It also tells us that it is likely that a giant meteorite landed on Earth, and also that the climate was cooling. But science cannot tell us just how quickly the dinosaurs died out, or whether it was a meteorite impact or climate change that actually killed them.

Even the experts cannot be sure how the dinosaurs died out. Most think that one of the two main theories – the impact theory or the **habitat** loss theory – could be correct, or that the dinosaurs were slowly dying out before they were finished off by a meteorite.

The tuatara is a species of reptile that has survived since the Jurassic period. Could some dinosaurs have survived, too?

What is certain is that there is plenty more to find out, and that we only know a tiny fraction of what there is to know about the dinosaurs. Our knowledge is getting better all the time as new **fossils** are found. Perhaps proof for one of the theories will be found soon.

What do you think?

Now that you have read about the scientific investigations into the death of the dinosaurs, can you draw any conclusions?

Bits of space dust hurtle into the atmosphere every day, causing shooting stars. Did a big lump of rock from space wipe out the dinosaurs?

Do you think that one of the two main theories is more likely than the other? Perhaps you prefer the impact theory because it is more exciting! What about some of the other theories? Do you think you can dismiss them just because they seem unlikely? Remember, there's no evidence to say they are not true. Do you have any theories of your own about what killed the dinosaurs?

Try to keep an open mind. Bear in mind that if scientists throughout history had not bothered to investigate things that appeared to be strange or mysterious, many scientific discoveries may never have been made.

Glossary

acid rain rain that is slightly acidic, formed when gases such as sulphur dioxide dissolve in water in the atmosphere

anomaly something that is out of the ordinary or unusual

archosaurs group of reptiles that lived about 250 million years ago. They were the ancestors of the dinosaurs.

atmosphere blanket of gas that surrounds the Earth

carnivore animal that eats only meat

crater wide, shallow, dish-shaped hole in the surface of a planet or moon, made when a meteorite crashes into the surface

eroded describes rocks that have been worn away by the actions of flowing water, wind or ice

evolve gradually develop new species of animals and plants over millions of years

extinct describes a species of animal or plant that is no longer living

fossil remains of an animal or plant that has been changed into rock after millions of years of being buried in the ground

geologist person who studies the rocks of the Earth's crust

habitat place where a species of animal or plant lives

herbivore animal that eats only plants

KT boundary time at the end of the Cretaceous period and the beginning of the Tertiary period, about 65 million years ago. This is when the dinosaurs died out.

methane gas that occurs naturally under the ground and is also made when plants rot or are digested by animals

minerals chemicals from which rocks are made

ozone layer layer of the gas ozone (a form of oxygen) in the upper atmosphere. The ozone layer stops harmful ultraviolet radiation from reaching the Earth's surface.

palaeontologist scientist who studies fossils of animals and plants that lived millions of years ago

predator animal that hunts other animals for food

radiometric way of finding the age of a piece of rock by measuring the amount of radiation coming from it

reptile one of a group of animals that have scaly skin and are cold-blooded. Lizards, snakes, crocodiles and dinosaurs are all reptiles.

sediment mud, sand and small pieces of rock that are washed down a river and then settle on the river bed or sea bed

sedimentary rocks rocks that are formed when layers of sediment are buried deep underground

silt sediment that is made of very tiny particles of rock. Silt is smoother than sand.

Solar System our Sun and the family of planets and moons that orbit around it

sub-tropical type of climate. In a sub-tropical climate, the temperature is always warm and there are dry seasons and seasons of heavy rain.

sunspot area on the Sun's surface that looks dark because it is cooler than the rest of the surface

supernova massive explosion that happens when a large star comes to the end of its life

supersonic faster than the speed of sound

Index